Angel in a Dog Suit ™

From the Inspiring & Entertaining

SCRiBBLE&grin ™

COLLECTION

Angel in a Dog Suit ™

From the Inspiring & Entertaining

SCRiBBLE&grin ™
COLLECTION

written by Mary Giuffre
scribbles by Paul L. Clark

published by

inspirtainment ink ™

Opening Imaginations to Dream Bigger!

Published in 2015 by inspirtainment ink
P.O. Box 565 Bewdley, ON, Canada, K0L 1E0
info@inspirtainment.com
www.ScribbleAndGrin.com
www.inspirtainment.com

Discounts on bulk quantities are available to schools, corporations,
professional associations, charities and other qualified organizations.
Please contact inspirtainment ink for details.

Library and Archives Canada Cataloguing in Publication

Giuffre, Mary
Clark, Paul L.
Scribble & Grin: Angel in a Dog Suit
Summary: Inspiration in rhyme. A true story that proves even the most
challenging times can become triumphs, that in adversity there is always
an opportunity for growth, and that when we don't give up on love,
life gets better.

Hardcover edition
ISBN: 978-0-9919101-5-1

Electronic edition - eBook
ISBN: 978-0-9919101-7-5

Printed and bound in the United States of America
Cover design, interior book design and formatting by Paul L.Clark

DEDICATION

For Jo Giuffre, who loved to hold Ruby on her knee
and who at eighty-eight, can still recite
the rhymes she learned as a child.
We love you Mom!

For Dr. Susan Gambling, Mary-Kay Lang-Lee, Marlene Marco
and for the staff and volunteers at
the Durham Region Humane Society, Ruby's story would not
have had such a happy ending without you.
Your dedication to the animals is appreciated!
Thank you!

For Raeanne MacDonald, who with a huge heart
at only twelve-years-old,
rescued Ruby's puppy mill sister Coco-Bear,
a spunky little girl with a badly injured leg.
Raeanne you're our hero!

PRECIOUS LIVES

Cherish a precious life today –
   Take more than a passing glance.
That pet's a stray or throw-away
   Who needs a second chance.

Save a precious life today –
   And share your forever home.
Pets want a lasting place to stay,
   So no one lives alone.

Adopt a precious life today –
   Give it a tender thought.
Just open up your heart and say,
   "My home's the perfect spot!"

Make lasting memories and change lives. Visit iAdopt.ca or your local SPCA or Humane Society.

Animal Welfare is everyone's responsibility.
Support your local SPCA or Humane Society by volunteering, donating or adopting.

A PROGRAM OF THE ONTARIO SPCA

FOREWORD

Few of life's joys compare to the warm connection we feel with animals. As the Chief Inspector of the Ontario SPCA, one of Canada's largest Animal Welfare organizations, everyday I see animals that are in need of help, care, and often a loving home.

Adoption is a life changing experience, for both the adopter and the animal in need. Mary Giuffre and Paul L. Clark have truly captured what it means to connect with an animal and how this connection not only affects the animal, but also the adopter.

Reaching both heart and mind 'Angel in a Dog Suit' is more than just an adoption story. A key to preventing animal cruelty, Humane Education is an Ontario SPCA priority and our programs empower youth to become informed, compassionate advocates for Animal Welfare. This book is an important addition to our Humane Education programs as it provides an opportunity for teachers and caregivers to help children connect to their own feelings about animals and about life itself.

The stories we share of animals that need love and support, and the ways these pets have changed the lives of their new families are like no other. There are many animals, like Ruby, waiting at the local shelter for a family and new home. The Ontario SPCA asks that you consider adoption; make lasting memories and change lives.

Connie Mallory, Chief Inspector
Ontario SPCA
iAdopt.ca | Ontariospca.ca

Angel in a Dog Suit is proudly endorsed by

In a cage, in a barn
        On a down-trodden farm,
A tiny gray dog
        Sat trembling from harm.

Though gentle and tame,
    No one gave her a name
And nobody cared
    When the mean people came.

The dog kept very still
        In that HUGE puppy mill.
She was hungry and thirsty,
            It made her feel ill.

    Always quiet and shaking
    Her poor heart was aching,
"Can't anyone see
    The mistakes they are making?"

There were hundreds of others,
        Most of them mothers
And she waited six years
With her sisters and brothers.

    In the dark she would pray
Until one sunny day,
Light burst through the door
        And swept them away!

To a shelter they **went**
  And to soothe her **torment**,
They fed her and bathed her
  But she wasn't **content**.

Despite fear and confusion,
This was **not** an **illusion**.
"Well, it IS better here."
Was her grateful **conclusion**.

While she stayed in their yard,
    The dog still felt on guard.
Though the spaces were larger
    The gates were still barred.

Many people would come
And she often felt dumb,
'cause they'd stare in her cage
    So the poor pup went numb.

Until one woman **came**
  And exclaimed, "What a **shame!**
You're an Angel sweet girl
    And you need a **name!**"

  She lifted her gently
  And listened intently,
To the dog's nervous heart
    Then spoke **confidently.**

"Hello precious stone
      Please don't sit here alone...
May I call you Ruby
            And give you a home?"

So that lady came back
   Each day with a snack
She called, "Come Ruby! Cheese!"
      And the pup left her pack!

Then together they'd walk
    And the lady would talk.
Ruby learned to climb curbs
    Then she tried out the block!

"Please come home with me.
 Where you will be free!"
You'll be part of our family.
    Oh won't you agree?"

So in love with her charms
          Ruby jumped in her **arms!**
She knew she was safe.
          No more nasty dog **farms!**

  Asleep on her knee
  Ruby's heart filled with glee,
And she dreamed lovely dreams
          Of the things she might **see!**

There were flowers and fishes
        With hearts full of wishes.
When she woke up at home
        She had her own dishes!

There was one bowl with food
And the other she viewed,
Was filled with cool water
        When it suited her mood!

At her house was a man,
         Who was part of the clan.
She was frightened at first.
         When she saw him she ran!

    She'd just watch and he'd wait,
    While she'd contemplate
Her eyes staring back,
         "Was this a mistake?"

But it didn't take long
         'til the two formed a bond,
'cause he'd toss her nice treats
    And she knew she belonged.

As they went through their day,
Near the lady she'd stay.
"Where's Ruby?" "Look down!"
            The man always would say!

Everyday in no rush,
            With a comb and a brush
The lady would groom her
            And Ruby was mush!

With the couple she'd walk,
        By the lake, to the dock.
'Til she built up her strength,
        She was carried a lot!

When she needed to rest
Ruby'd scratch up a nest,
In her pocket-dog basket,
        "Ahhh! This is the best!"

Very quiet and meek
        Ruby never would speak.
Then one day in the yard
Out a happy "WOOF" squeaked!

    She soon learned to run.
    So she'd do it for fun!
In wide figure-eights
            Until she was done!

There were so many joys
        Like her own squeaky toys!
She'd jump and she'd play,
            "Oh I so love the noise!"

She forgot all her fright,
'cause they sang day and night!
Making up silly nicknames
                To Ruby's delight!

And as days stretched ahead
              Ruby slept on their bed,
With her very own blanket
              Of yellow and red.

She lounged in the sunshine
With all things aligned.
Her troubles were over,
              "This family is MINE!"

"Sweet Ruby, whenever
   You're scared please don't ever
Forget that we promised
      To love you forever!"

Well her tail wagged around,
Then she flipped upside down!
'cause she loved them right back
   From her toes to her crown!

Feeling comfy and warm,
        She began to transform
And then Ruby's gray dog suit
                Took on a new form.

    Her soft coat would flow
    With a silvery glow,
As her sweet inner Angel
            Was starting to show!

Very soon you could tell
    She'd come out of her shell!
With each person she'd meet
    Her wee heart would swell!

And wherever she went
You'd hear people comment,
"She has something special
    She looks heaven sent!"

Ruby felt so **relieved**
    With each smile she **received**.
As love spread 'cross their faces,
            She knew and **believed**.

    "I never gave up!"
    Thought this brave little pup.
"My heart's open wide
            To love people close **up!**"

With the husband and wife,
　　Tender care replaced strife.
So Ruby knew peace
　　　For the rest of her life.

　Her heart was courageous!
　Her spirit – vivacious!
And above all, her LOVE
　　Was Divine and contagious!

AFTERWORD

This is a true story.

A puppy mill survivor, Ruby came into our lives on April 19, 2012,
when we offered video services to the Humane Society
to assist in the adoption of 125 puppy mill dogs in their care.

A sweeter being has not graced the planet.

Her health was seriously compromised by the horrible affects
of six caged years and our two years together passed
much too quickly. Despite best efforts, Ruby took her place
among the Angels on March 10, 2014.

It's said that rubies are Divine LOVE in crystal form.
Ruby brought so much joy to the lives she touched
~ surely Divine LOVE in doggy form!

We believe her inner Angel just got too big for her dog suit
so she's off spreading LOVE across the universe.

We miss you Sweet Girl!

From the Heart
~ Mary & Paul

OUR 'ANGEL' INVESTORS

People like you who opened their heart.

Tim Arenburg & Charmaine Hoet

Georgina Madott, Bertha Madott, Clare Kosnik, Anthony Madott

Anna Marie Kalcevich, Beatrice O'Connor,
Octavia O'Connor, Simone Bergh, Sebastian Bergh

Joe & Mary Giuffre

Jo Giuffre

Denise & Peter Brazolot

Anna-Marie & Don Heitzner & dogs: Schautze & Reggie

Janis & Phil Aitken

Debbie & Frank Covelli

Alva Folkes

Divine Light Spiritual Foundation

Mark Shekter & Nancy Trites Botkin

Donna & Roger Cole, Tyler Samuel Ross, Emily Cole Ross,
William Cole Linton, Julia Elizabeth Linton

Shirley & Don Bankey, Kolby Bankey, Lily Bankey,
Liam Thomson, Brody Thomson, Foster the Cat

Marnie MacDonald & dogs: Panda, Jack, Bailey, Holly & Coco

Brent Marchant & Trevor Laster

Monika Horvat & Tommy the Cat

Cheri Anderson

Carol Johnston & puppy mill survivors: Molly, Dixie, Lexi, Davey & Gizmo

Amanda D'Attolico, Alexander D'Attolico

Jaya Kochanoff

Roxanne McDonald

Janice Groom

SamisGunn's Jessie the Chessie

Mystical Gatherings

Dagmar Schoenrock, Tinara Herpel, Melanie Herpel,
Percy the Chihuahua

Jane Saracino & Emily the Yorkie

Olivia Garstin Collier

Gabrielle Brown

Shannon Sheppard

In Loving Memory

...of our own furry family-members:

Pepper
Mucker
Baja
Rhea
Gemini
Blue
Jade
Ruby

ABOUT THE AUTHORS

Mary Giuffre & Paul L. Clark R.G.D.

Internationally recognized television and film professionals for 30+ years, Mary Giuffre and Paul L. Clark stepped out of mainstream media to work from the heart.

Mary's intrigue with TV began in childhood, watching endless hours of programming, an interest she turned into an award-winning career in family-friendly television. Passionate about inspiring people to live heart-centered lives, Mary is now an independent producer, director, editor, writer and children's author.

From animation and special FX to graphic design and fine art, Paul is an artist in every sense of the word. His award-winning career has led him to writing, creating and designing children's content, including the `Scribble & Grin Collection`.

Creative partners, married for 25+ years, Mary and Paul live with their little dogs Matilda & Roxie, by Rice Lake in the beautiful rolling hills of Northumberland County, Ontario, Canada.

OTHER BOOKS created & written by Mary Giuffre and Paul L. Clark

Translated to Braille

Collectable Hardcover Edition
If you are unable to purchase this book from your local bookseller,
provide them with this title and number, so they can order it for you!
Scribble & Grin: 53 Rhymes for Inspiring Times
ISBN: 978-0-9919101-0-6
or
Order online through our Scribble & Grin website below.

BULK orders are also available at a discounted price.
Please see our publisher's contact information below for details.

eBook Edition
This book is also available in all eBook formats.
Scribble & Grin: 53 Rhymes for Inspiring Times
ISBN: 978-0-9919101-1-3
Available for order through our website below,
as well as most online book retailers.

Braille Edition
This book is available in Braille format.
Scribble & Grin: 53 Rhymes for Inspiring Times
Contracted ISBN: 978-0-9919101-4-4
Uncontracted UEB ISBN: 978-0-9919101-2-0
Contracted UEB ISBN: 978-0-9919101-3-7
Available for order through our website below,

Our official website [not case-sensitive]
www.ScribbleAndGrin.com

How To Order This Book

Collectable Hard Cover Edition

If you are unable to purchase this book from your local bookseller,
provide them with this title and number, so they can order it for you!

Scribble & Grin: Angel in a Dog Suit
ISBN: 978-0-9919101-5-1

or

Order online through our Scribble & Grin website below.

BULK orders are also available at a discounted price.
Please see our publisher's contact information below for details.

eBook Edition

This book is also available in iPad format.

Scribble & Grin: Angel in a Dog Suit
ISBN: 978-0-9919101-7-5

Available for order through our website below,
as well as the Apple Store.

Our official website [not case-sensitive]
www.ScribbleAndGrin.com

How To Get In Touch

We love to hear from our readers, so tell us what you think!
If you have comments, stories or questions for Mary and Paul,
you're welcome to contact us through our publisher.

Publisher:
inspirtainment ink
P.O. Box 565 Bewdley, Ontario, Canada
K0L 1E0
Email: info@inspirtainment.com
Website: www.inspirtainment.com

inspirtainment ink ™
Opening Imaginations to Dream Bigger!

CPSIA information can be obtained
at www.ICGtesting.com
Printed in the USA
LVHW07*1340031018
592270LV00014B/61/P